Become that leader

Foundation for effective leadership (mysteries to great leadership)

Emma K. Laniar

Table of contents

Chapter 1

realize your strengths and tools as a leader (influence and authority)

You've reached a stage in your career when leadership experience is vital to you. But what follows next? Beyond selecting what sort of leader you want to be, it's important to think about the notion of power vs influence.

For many, a position of leadership corresponds to dominance over others.

But there's much more to leadership than authority and power. This style of one-dimensional leadership may create short-term gains. In the long run, it won't help you win the trust and respect of the people you lead.

There is a range of various management styles that leaders may examine and pick the one that suits them best.

Over the long run, possessing influence that goes deeper than the surface counts. That is if you want to establish a high-performing and loyal staff.

This is where power and influence come into play. Both are key practices in building a legacy of leadership.

Influence:
Leadership is a process wherein a person encourages a group of others to strive toward the attainment of a shared objective that they think is desirable. Thus, influence is vital to good leadership. Getting others to follow is the sine qua non of leadership. Leaders get things done via others. They motivate and coach people toward goal fulfillment and continuously build and keep cooperative working relationships.

Over the last few decades, experimental psychologists have learned which approaches regularly induce individuals to yield, cooperate, or change.

Their research demonstrates that influence is regulated by various principles that may be taught and utilized. Some of the concepts include credibility, reciprocity, attractiveness, colleagueship, and commitment. Leaders must also have the competence to address problems, have a sense of justice in dealing with situations and employees, be positive and show self-efficacy. Leaders need to sell ideas and persuade individuals to support and execute choices.

To be genuinely successful — in good times and in times of tremendous struggle — leaders must possess the capacity to influence people.

By definition, influence is the capacity to alter the behavior of others in a specific way, using essential methods that include, connect, and inspire people.

Influence is not to be mistaken with power or control. It's not about manipulating people to get your way. It's about identifying what encourages employee dedication and leveraging that information to leverage performance and good outcomes.

A leader's capacity to influence others is founded on trust; in fact, our influence expands in proportion to the amount of trust that exists in a connection. Let's take a look at how leaders successfully develop trust and improve their influence on others.

Without the competence and capacity to influence others, the genuinely essential things in business and life can't be done.

But good leaders don't simply command; they inspire, convince, and encourage. Leaders use the knowledge and talents of a group, direct members toward a shared objective and agreement, and bring forth a commitment to accomplishing outcomes.

4 keys required to influence others
1. Practice "Organizational Intelligence."
All companies have 2 sides: the official structure shown on the org chart and the informal structure, which more commonly mirrors how

things truly get done. Politically smart leaders understand both.

Political awareness is both a mentality and a competence. Savvy executives understand politics as a neutral and essential component of company life that can be utilized constructively and ethically to accomplish organizational purposes.

For a leader, political wisdom in action looks like this:

Networking to increase social capital, especially mixing strategically.

Thinking before reacting, analyzing context and aims before selecting when and how to share their point of view.

Paying focused attention to nonverbal signs, exercising active listening, contemplating how others may feel, and finding methods to appeal to the common good.

Leaving people with a nice impression, without coming off as "trying too hard."

Learn the 6 critical skills you need to be more politically informed.

2. Promote Yourself, Promote Your Team.

Self-promotion is sometimes perceived as boasting or selfishness. But effective leaders realize that by marketing themselves honestly, for the right reasons, they can pierce through the information that bombards us all each day.

In the hands of a smart leader, self-promotion isn't only a tool to further one's career. It may create exposure and opportunity for their direct reports, promote the team and organizational pride, and make talents and ideas more evident throughout the business – eventually boosting cooperation and consensus.

Two self-promotion tactics stand out.

First, leaders are effective at persuading people to discover methods to collect an audience. They may ask additional individuals to be part of a team, project, or problem-solving process.

Second, they find methods to "put on a show" and step into the limelight at chosen gatherings and meetings, sometimes establishing their events. Learn more about why you should concentrate on successful, real self-promotion.

3. Build & Maintain a Foundation of Trust.

Building and retaining trust is key for leadership. Without trust, leaders may be able to compel individuals to obey, but they'll never harness the full dedication, talents, and creativity the group can give. Leveraging these assets is crucial when facing challenging issues or implementing strategic change, thus trust is vital.

People yearn for leaders who can recognize their vulnerabilities and inspire them, understand them, encourage them, and navigate them through the oncoming catastrophe. This requires the leader to display a wide variety of knowledge and actions, some of which could appear contradictory, but when applied in an appropriate and timely way, create circumstances that build trust.

Trust demands a fine balance between pushing individuals into areas where they're uncomfortable while also listening intently to their worries and opinions. Among the various "balancing acts" they must seek to maintain, trustworthy leaders navigate between harshness and empathy as people struggle with transformation, as well as the urgency with patience as change unfolds. Learn more about ways to develop leadership trust.

4. Leverage Networks.
Finally, leaders with competence in influencing others realize and harness the potential of networks. Organizations are more dynamic; they evolve in size and form over time. Influential leaders know that their networks must also be dynamic, and they consistently expand and enhance their networks. They're also savvy in choosing how and when to tap into this network.

Power and authority:While power and authority might appear similar in ordinary English, they are independent ideas. Both authority and power are vital to consider for successful leadership since leaders can change values that shape actions.
  Power refers to the capacity or possibility for a person to influence others and regulate their conduct. For example, a boss of a firm can put up rules for the organization's everyday running.

Authority refers to the legal and formal authority to deliver instructions and make decisions. For example, a manager has the right to alter workers' work schedules depending on the requirements of the organization.

Many leadership development programs address the delicate balancing act that is frequently necessary for leaders. Leaders have authority, but they also have duties.

Leadership is in many ways a balancing act.

Leaders also have authority, which is both something that is defined by people higher up and a personal trait based on influence and personal connections. How they wield power and authority considerably influences their performance as leaders.

I have dealt with leadership coaching clients that conflate power with authority and as a consequence, lead less effectively. I believe that understanding the differences between the two can help in understanding the roles and responsibilities of leaders.

A leader is someone who has the ability and/ or authority to influence others' actions. How these factors are employed will be different for various leadership styles. These leadership styles have varied benefits and downsides, their success may be modified by the qualities of the leader, the work at hand, and the members of the team.

Leaders Need Both Power and Authority
Power is something fundamental. It is frequently more effective in the shorter term. In World War II, for example, the Allies possessed the potential to liberate Paris by driving the Germans out. Sometimes power is necessary and appropriate. Most of us would use our physical might to grab a youngster out of the path of an oncoming automobile, for example.

There's no question that sometimes the exercise of power is necessary.
Authority is also important for leadership. Because of their decisiveness, achievement track record, influence, bravery, and inspiration,

exceptional leaders can assist their teams to accomplish great things.

Great leaders may have power, but they are more likely to keep it in reserve and depend on authority to lead.

But excellent leaders recognize when circumstances compel the use of authority. Such a boss, for example, won't hesitate to terminate someone for gross wrongdoing.

How to Leverage Power, authority, and Leadership Effectively

All in all, our study results imply that leaders may be more successful when they stress the power of connections and the power of knowledge, and also expand their other potential sources of power.

Here are some techniques for utilizing power and authority in leadership effectively:

1. Make connections a priority. Your capacity to leverage the power of relationships will be limited if you're not connecting with the proper individuals. Therefore, identify the individuals with whom you need to create or grow a

connection, and put time and attention into your current relationships.

Seek to understand people better and appreciate others' needs to create the social capital necessary to influence others now and in the future.

Repair broken connections and the impression people may have of you. Look for methods to restore trust with individuals via face-to-face engagement and the giving of honest criticism. Be conscious of how people view you and search for methods to modify their opinions by requesting input from trustworthy individuals.

2. Don't overplay your agenda. While the power of connections may be a successful strategy for advancing your agenda, it also risks people considering you as self-serving rather than a "team player." Leaders must be aware of these unfavorable impressions to properly use the power of connections. Ensure that pursuing your agenda is not regarded as an abuse of authority.

3. Maximize your communication network. Think about the folks you communicate with the most. Are they giving you access to unique information or repetitive information? Expand your network to locate individuals who may be untapped sources of knowledge.

4. Be liberal with information. If you are a key node or conduit of information, remember that keeping knowledge to yourself might have negative implications. Share information openly and with honesty. You don't want to be viewed as hoarding knowledge for your advantage. Of course, you don't want to make the opposite error and divulge private or personal information.

5. Make the most of your situation. Research and experience demonstrate that authority doesn't inherently accompany a formal leadership job. We can all think of colleagues who, despite their parallels in tenure and position, may have more or less influence than we do. In other words, status doesn't necessarily imply power. You may

wish to find some subtle methods to signal your official authority, such as inserting your title in your email signature, talking in meetings where you generally remain quiet or adjusting your style of clothing so that you resemble those at the level above you. This is also a fantastic example of efficient self-promotion at work.

6. Develop your brand of charisma. How would you feel if you were in an audience where your generally low-key CEO "borrowed" the manner of an exuberant, larger-than-life motivational speaker? At best you could be amused; at worst, you would perceive the CEO as a pitiful approximation of the real thing.

Regardless of your degree of charisma, the objective is to make tiny modifications to your leadership image while preserving your genuineness.

Maintain the attributes that make you who you are, but attempt to find 2 or 3 actions that can boost your capacity to interact with people (such as making more eye contact, smiling more frequently) (such as making more eye contact, smiling more often). Practice those new habits, obtaining guidance from a coach or mentor if required.

7. Be the expert. Perhaps the most intriguing thing about power is that it's typically in the eyes of the beholder. You can't merely have power de facto unless there are people prepared to view you as having power. The same holds for expert power — it comes from genuine competence (such as an advanced degree or appropriate experience) or the impression of expertise. Don't be hesitant about presenting your qualifications on your business cards, in your email signature, on social media, or talking about your experience and expertise.

8. Tailor your authority to reward others. Many leaders incorrectly feel that leveraging reward authority solely implies giving employees more money. While this alternative seems enticing, it's not always attainable. Consider acknowledging and rewarding your team members in different ways.

Ask your team members what they would find gratifying. Some team members may find a group picnic or excursion incredibly gratifying; others may find this monotonous or exhausting. Time off or flexible hours could work for some workers; others may not even take note. Whatever their motive, don't make the mistake of presuming that one reward fits all.

9. Reward with words. Give favorable remarks frequently. Our experience with leaders across sectors tells us that throughout a normal working relationship, it requires a ratio of 4:1 (4 positives for every negative) for a receiver of feedback to think that the feedback has been fair. This does not imply that you have to offer a team member 4 positive pieces of feedback every time you have a bad message to share.

It does show that many of us have a long way to go in terms of recognizing what our staff is doing properly.

At the same time, when team members fail to live up to expectations, communicate and enforce your standards, but be sure to provide support along the way. We recommend using SBI to provide feedback in a talent conversation. Also, be transparent about repercussions for conduct or outcomes that don't match expectations — and follow through consistently.

10. Teach others. Leveraging your entire power doesn't simply hoard it. If you want to empower the people you lead, you also need to educate them on how to utilize the authority they have available to them. Think about the individuals you lead. What are those at the top of the list doing effectively? What might folks at the bottom of the list be doing better?

Earned leadership may be a beautiful thing. Unfortunately, there will always be leaders who use their position to abuse power, and although they may make things happen in the short term, they lose out over the long run.

These leaders, who know when power must be utilized and when it should be kept in reserve, are the ones who stand to achieve the most over the long run.

Chapter 2

emphasize personal development

Simply said, having a personal growth plan enhances the probability that life will move precisely.

How should we prioritize personal development? By taking the time to create and aim for our objectives (you can call them resolutions if you want to, but I like to call them "life goals").

Setting life objectives may better your professional possibilities, raise your self-confidence, and lead to a more rewarding existence. This form of goal planning may be used in practically every aspect of your personal life - from health and wellbeing to education, to job aspirations.

Your Personal Development Plan:
Define what you desire (take some time with this one - dream a bit and come up with a rough list. Then go specific, i.e. train for a certain career,

drop 15 pounds, go back to school and acquire your degree, etc.)

If you have numerous objectives; arrange them in order of the ones you expect to attain first, second, and so on.

In this phase, identify the abilities you already have and those that are missing and consequently, hindering you from accomplishing your objective. Jot all of them down.

Define why you want it (what will the advantages be? What will you gain?)

Visualizing what success will look and feel like is vital. Consider developing a vision board to keep you motivated and on track. Include photographs of a happier, healthier self!

Define how you intend to get there (this is the most essential phase - what will it take? Upskilling? Seeing a nutritionist? Taking online courses?

These should be actionable events — signing up for a course in a skill for which you require improvement, for example.

Before you take action, prepare how you are going to assess your progress. Make sure to add tiny milestones along the road so that you may celebrate little accomplishments.

Keep a list of sources of inspiration and support at the ready. These are folks who you may depend on when things could become hard; or uplifting reading material or podcasts. Anything that stimulates you and drives you ahead will do! Set a deadline. A goal without a strategy is simply a desire. Set a time to review your progress. If required, rework your strategy and timeframe and start over!
"

To attain your objectives, you will need to plan ahead and actively seek personal development opportunities. Mapping out the process will help you to monitor your development and push you to remain on track.
"Learn to work harder on yourself than you do on your career."
This one piece of advice is so vital that if you don't follow it, your prospects for long-term

success in your work and your life are severely lowered.

You need to be strong as a person to be a successful leader and have the biggest beneficial influence.

This means, that while you're putting out fires and managing the people on your team, you have to continually work on who you are.

You may absorb tremendous quantities of knowledge on managing people and reacting to stressful circumstances. But utilizing this information may be incredibly tough. That's because the world you live in is a continual onslaught of hurdles and failures. It requires guts, commitment, and a variety of other inner traits to follow through and truly execute what you learned.

So you have to be clever, and you have to be strong—at the heart of who you are.

But this isn't simple, for two reasons:

#1 - The essential abilities you need aren't explicitly taught in schools.

You learn traits like bravery, persistence, self-discipline, effort, responsibility, and integrity from life experience, but generally not in a systematic fashion. If you were fortunate, you received important counsel from your parents, teachers, coaches, and other adult mentors.

Most likely, however, you didn't always have great role models. Some of what you learned along the road was the incorrect stuff—habits that don't benefit you today when the going gets tough.

It would be lovely if you could click a "delete" key in your brain and remove the habits that come in your way - and simply replace them with the abilities you need.

But that's not how it works in the actual world.

#2 – Your brain is hard-wired from years of programming.

Your brain doesn't discriminate good information from negative input. It doesn't protect you from yourself. It doesn't say, "Uh, Chuck, my guy, I'm sorry I can't program that for you. It'll get you in problems down the road."

No, when you repeat a behavior frequently enough, your brain simply goes ahead and ingrains it as a habit.
So you might wind up with an addiction. Or behave like a jerk. Or prevent contentious situations with clients, colleagues, and loved ones.
And it's because, through time, your brain cells established real physical connections and built the networks in your brain that permit your behavior. Your existing manner of doing things is hard-wired.

A super highway simile
Think about a habit you have currently that's generating troubles for you.
It's a lot like a familiar, well-traveled path. After so many years of experience, the turns and stops

are nearly instinctive. But at some point, you discover that the road you've been traveling has some potholes. It's holding you back and slowing you down.

So you decide to make a change and try something that works better.

This is like attempting to create a whole new super-highway. The construction is going to take time since you're beginning with a dirt road. It's going to be a rocky, unpleasant journey at first since the new habit seems odd.

That implies, that when you attempt to break a behavior, at first your outcomes may go worse before they get better. Sometimes you'll forget what to do. Or you'll make errors. You might wind up feeling embarrassed, disillusioned, and upset.

To get to that efficient road, you have to continue through the building period. You essentially have to rewire your brain by making new connections, and this takes time. It might take weeks or months, depending on the intricacy of what you're attempting to alter. Progress might be sluggish and unpleasant. When failures arise, you'll be tempted to go back to the way you know so well.

And that's precisely what occurs with many leaders.

When a new strategy appears too hard, individuals default to employing the established habit. They know what they should be doing and they know the old system produces trouble, but they aren't prepared to pay the price to change.

So how do you ever go from that dirt road to the superhighway?

To break out of your comfort zone, you've got to have a strong commitment to your growth - to work on yourself until you've accomplished the change you want to make.

You have to be ready to suffer discomfort as you advance from conscious competence – knowing what to do – to unconscious competence – being able to execute it instinctively. If you simply stay with it, the brain will rewire itself and you'll ultimately cease utilizing the old path completely.

Following these three stages will help you get past the difficult building period.

STEP 1 – FOCUS

Most leaders have a lot of irons in the fire. Managing tremendous activity on numerous fronts may bring you amazing outcomes.

But that attitude doesn't work when it comes to your growth. You can't tackle numerous personal changes concurrently if you want them to become lasting. Your brain simply doesn't operate that way.

Instead, you need to have a laser focus. Take a long hard look at yourself and find the ONE item that keeps tripping you up. These few questions may stir your thinking…

Do you frequently pursue bright flashy goods that distract you from your main priorities?

Are you afraid to contact those who may help you advance further in your job because you lack self-confidence?

Do you quit up at the first indication of rejection or resistance?

Do disappointments and defeats put you in such a depression that you lose momentum for days or weeks?

Do you prefer to wait for things to come to you instead of taking initiative?

If you're not sure what you need to improve on most, simply ask the individuals who know you well. They can see what you can't. Be courteous when you hear the truth about yourself – and appreciate them for their honesty.

STEP 2 – TAKE ACTION

Once you decide something to work on – and figure out how to do it effectively – it's time to take action. You've got to implement what you learn — at work and home.

And not just once or twice. Dozens or perhaps hundreds of times. Remember, you're making new physical connections in your brain. It takes a lot of repetition and practice to develop that super-highway.

STEP 3 – REFLECT

You expedite the process when you take time to think about what you learned each time you practice the new habit.

With everything going on in a busy leader's life, who has time to pause and think about what's happened?

YOU do…

because otherwise you'll keep making the same errors and never learn from them. That's what generally occurs. People move from one thing to another without taking away the lessons from each experience.

So what precisely should you think about? What does "reflection" look like?

Take a few minutes to ask yourself these 5 crucial questions after each event, and you'll be shocked at the insights you obtain.

What occurred and how do you feel about it?
Why did it happen that way?
What were the consequences?
What will you do differently in the future?
What are your next steps?
If you commit to practicing this cycle of focus-action-reflection while you work on your personal growth, you will re-wire your brain. You'll gain the qualities you need to succeed in the competitive and demanding world of a leader.

Chapter 3

serve: servant leadership

Servant Leadership is one the most effective methods to create a good influence on your company and the individuals inside it. We have all heard the adage "Lead By Example," but Servant Leadership takes leading by example to the next level.

Leadership is about learning, growing, and helping others.

Servant leaders concentrate on the needs of others instead of command and control. Servant leadership provides self-expression, personal growth, a feeling of community, and ownership. Valuing, appreciating, and inspiring your staff is the basis of a servant leader

Servant leadership is a leadership paradigm in which the objective of the leader is to serve. This is distinct from conventional leadership when the leader's primary goal is the prospering of their firm or organization. A servant leader shares authority puts the needs of the workers first and helps individuals grow and perform as highly as possible.

[1] Instead of the people laboring to serve the leader, the leader exists to serve the people.
[2]When leaders adjust their perspective and serve first, they benefit as well as their workers in that their people gain personal development, while the company develops as well due to the employees' increased dedication and engagement. Since this leadership style came around, a lot of different organizations[example required] have chosen this method as their manner of leadership.

Being a serving leader has been claimed to be the finest form of leader that you can be. The issue is, how do you know that you are a serving leader? Servant leadership characteristics are well-known, but how can we keep ourselves in line and on track?
Well, the solution is more clear than you may expect. With so much written and shared about

serving leaders and their traits, obtaining a clear picture of your route to becoming a serving leader is rather straightforward.

Ways to assist people as a leader

Listen:

So few of us genuinely feel listened to on any given day - in every element of our lives, not just at work. When we genuinely listen to individuals we are: satisfying a vital internal need, improving our connection with them, adding to the levels of trust, and obtaining information, perspective, and ideas that may progress us towards the objectives we are attempting to attain.

How did you listen yesterday and how would you improve on that today?

Respond:

People want us to listen because they want to be heard. As a leader, we are asked questions about processes and procedures, ideas, obstacles, resources and so much more. For people to feel heard, we must react. Perhaps our response may not always be the one they hoped for, but from a standpoint of helping people, we lead we must reply to their inquiries and demands.

Are you responding to all queries and emails in a timely (as defined by the asker/sender) manner?

Engage:

Engaging might be seen as combining listening and reacting together, but I mean something far more than basic mathematics. This notion isn't about the crucial (but popular) idea of engaging people.

This is about gazing in the mirror. Are you engaged with those you lead? Do you share with them, hold talks with them, and in general interact with them outside the typical discourse of your profession.

Are you proactively connecting with the people you lead every day?

Ask:

Do you truly want to know how others are feeling? Do you truly want their ideas? Do you feel they have strategies to impact higher results? If you do, when did you last ask? If you don't, reevaluate your response. Still not convinced? How do you feel when someone asks you a question?

Who (and what) will you ask right now?

Care:

When you think about individuals helping others, wouldn't you agree that behind all of the behaviors and acts is a feeling of caring? When we care about the people we lead, we are serving them.

When we care about who they are, their goals and objectives, their beliefs, and their issues, we are serving them.

This type of compassion doesn't imply we need to (or should) become everyone's closest friend. It implies that we care about them; the person-to-person actual compassion.

Done from the heart, acts of care and generosity may make more of a difference in your overall outcomes and productivity than any process plan, Gantt chart, or scoping document.

Do you care, and can others detect it from your actions?

While they may seem like "soft" or "touchy-feely" recommendations, that couldn't be farther from the truth. When incorporated as a genuine component of your leadership strategy, they will make a tremendous impact in the lives of individuals you lead and any of the overall outcomes you produce.

Start serving today.

Potential Pointer: Once you grasp that leadership is an act of service to others you are better positioned for success. Everything you do as a leader may not be popular or agreed with, but when you remember your position of helping people in pursuit of worthwhile objectives, you will lead with better concentration, compassion, and success.

Servant leadership is vital because it fosters a caring atmosphere where people feel that they are recognized, appreciated, and respected. It may help firms establish healthier work environments with high employee morale and engagement.

By adopting the old paradigm of leadership, the outcome will likely be compliance and nothing more. Employees won't desire to go above and above. But by being compassionate, empathic, modest, and helping people, the company may prosper, and employees will feel empowered. This in turn enables greater growth across the company.

Chapter 4

be an empathetic or compassionate leader.

Empathy is a vital aspect of all leadership styles, from democratic to affiliative, since it is what enables us to make relationships and influence others.

An empathic leader shows a real interest in coworkers' lives, issues, and overall sentiments. They engage with others in a manner that leaves colleagues feeling appreciated and respected for their personal and professional merits.

This sort of leader attempts to comprehend their problems and what they are going through, to give support and aid. Empathy is a vital feature of servant leadership as well while not all empathetic leaders practice servant leadership.

Overall, an empathetic leader engages with people in a manner that leaves them feeling secure and cared for, and as if they have a relationship based on trust.

WHAT IS EMPATHETIC LEADERSHIP?

Empathetic leadership is a type of leadership that focuses on relating with people and understanding their points of view. Empathetic leaders show a real interest in the people around them - what makes them tick, what motivates them, and the way they feel.

They want to understand why people are the way they are, and this desire helps them become exceptional leaders who can connect with all sorts of people and modify their approach based on who they are talking with.

There are disadvantages to empathic leadership attributes. Empathetic leaders often find it difficult to confront people and deliver critical criticism. But the greatest empathetic leaders don't simply feel for their team members — they take action to help them improve their careers, and sometimes that involves providing constructive criticism.

WHY IS EMPATHY IMPORTANT IN LEADERSHIP?

Being an empathic leader isn't simply about emotions. Practicing empathy at work provides actual advantages for your team, your organization, and your career.

INCREASED TRUST
Building trust in the workplace isn't always simple – but when you fully understand the thoughts and requirements of your team, it becomes easier. By letting your staff know you are there for them and giving unconditional support, you'll establish an atmosphere where they feel they can come to you with anything.

STRONGER TEAMS
Empathetic leadership doesn't simply offer your employees trust in you but in each other. As Tony says, "Don't attempt to be flawless; just be a great example of being human." Leading by example is a top empathetic leadership attribute that helps you to develop successful teams.

BETTER DECISION MAKING
Empathetic leaders are attentive and receptive to the viewpoints, worldviews, and experiences of others. They have an insatiable curiosity and

know-how to ask the appropriate questions so that they are continuously learning new things. This helps individuals to better forecast the repercussions of their actions — and make challenging judgments fast and properly.

INCREASED INFLUENCE

Why is empathy crucial in leadership? It isn't only to help others. It may also help you personally. Empathetic leaders know how to engage, connect and obtain leverage that enables them to influence people in the future. This doesn't imply they are unethical. They simply know how to meet others' wants in a manner that benefits everyone involved.

MORE PROMOTIONS

It's no surprise that compassionate leadership leads to higher performance at work. This leadership style is perceived favorably by both employers and workers, resulting in favorable performance reports across the board and leading to more promotions and better contentment at work.

TOP FOUR EMPATHY LEADERSHIP TRAITS

There are numerous facets to being an empathic leader, as you must continuously adjust to people around you. But compassionate leaders consistently demonstrate these four attributes.

1. EMPATHY

The number one attribute of empathic leaders is of course empathy: the capacity to not just perceive others' feelings but to experience them as well. They achieve this by practicing deep listening, being present with people, and learning to understand and react to diverse working methods and communication styles. As Tony explains, "We are all different in the way we experience the world. We must utilize this knowledge as a guide to our communication with others." Empathetic leaders embody this ideal.

2. COMPASSION

What's the difference between empathy and compassion? Empathy is your capacity to sense others' sorrow, but compassion is your willingness to act on it and heal their suffering. Think of empathy as a data-gathering instrument, whereas compassion is putting what you've learned into practice. Empathy could assist you to discover what motivates your colleagues, which you can then put into practice to encourage them to provide a knockout performance.

3. EMOTIONAL INTELLIGENCE

Emotional intelligence is a key aspect of empathy, but like compassion, it is not the same thing. Emotional intelligence encompasses not just your capacity to perceive others' emotions but to identify and regulate your own emotions. This helps you to develop empathy and compassion without letting emotion get the better of you - a line that is vital to establish in empathetic leadership.

4. FLEXIBILITY

Empathetic leaders can swiftly assess the needs and emotions of people and adjust to any scenario - a quality that is particularly crucial to crisis leadership. Tony advises, "Keep dedicated to your decisions, but stay adaptable in your approach." The empathic leadership style succeeds at this, never wavering from their strong principles and convictions, while sincerely appreciating the perspectives of others and integrating them into their choices. This helps them to develop a culture of invention and creativity, where all ideas are considered.

Chapter 5

Be a good listener

Effective leaders are excellent listeners. When leaders first occupy a position of responsibility, taking the effort to hear and understand the individuals who make up a unit may help them create rapport and credibility from the get-go.

One effective technique among powerful and successful leaders is to engage in a listening and learning exercise when they first take over: spending the time to meet, talk with, and — most important — listen to the people inside the units or divisions they control.

Another focus point for listening and learning would be to evaluate your unit's strengths and deficiencies. You may then use the findings as to the foundation for a group chat or individual interviews. Faculty or staff members may all agree that a certain issue is a problem, but they could have quite diverse perspectives about what is causing that problem or how best to deal with it.

We all have the urge to be acknowledged in some manner. The best approach to identifying someone is by listening to them and embracing them the way they are. An excellent listener can perceive the world through the perspective of others. Listening allows us to grasp diverse sorts of perspectives and see the broader picture. This also assists us in directing individuals with varied personalities and talents towards a shared objective.

As a leader, you want to let your colleagues know that they are valued and liked - doing so plays a crucial part in helping them achieve their maximums. Listening has a big importance in this game.

Listening is a basic communication ability. It's crucial for successful leadership.

Leadership listening will be an increasingly crucial talent in the future. Organizations will put increased attention on employee experience.

Let's take a look at what makes a great listener, why excellent listening skills are essential in the digital era, and how to get better at listening as a leader.

The necessity of listening as a leader
The value of listening in leadership is vital for team effectiveness.

A boss that is dictatorial and judgemental may cause their people to be fearful of them and unable to communicate. This may lead to team dysfunction and low productivity.

So why are listening skills important? Here are five more ways that listening abilities make you a more successful leader:

1. Listening strengthens your potential as a leader
We can constantly learn from everyone around us, even our direct reports. Effective listening provides you with information and perspectives that strengthen your leadership potential.
Being receptive to criticism and fresh ideas from your team helps you learn and develop as a leader.

2. Listening shows you care

Listening to someone indicates you care about what they're saying and connect with their sentiments.

This promotes a work climate of trust. Having the trust of your staff provides you with more power over them.

At the same time, it makes people more driven and devoted to their tasks.

3. Listening helps you grasp the situation

If you fail to pay adequate attention to what your workers say, you will not completely comprehend the problem.

Failing to appreciate the issue may cause you to provide advice or suggestions that are unproductive or don't get to the source of the problem.

4. Listening helps you better understand your company

Listening to your staff is the greatest method to understand the demands of your customers and company.
This helps you create successful tactics that are targeted to the needs of your organization.

5. Listening provides you a glimpse of the reality on the ground
Listening provides you with information and insights into the day-to-day realities of your people.
It's crucial to develop an environment of trust and encourage your staff to talk frankly about their everyday issues.
You may be astonished at how different their reality is from your perspective of it.

Chapter 6

be an example of embracing change

Change, they say, is the only constant.

But if the change is so continuous and ubiquitous, then why do we oppose it? Why does it seem so hard to adapt to it?

This is because we are creatures of habit. We feel comfortable and confident in doing things the way we have always done them. A departure from the past–like a change of work or a relocation to a new town–makes us uneasy, even though we know it's a change for the best.

We make choices and establish objectives to modify habits often. However, how frequently are we genuinely able to modify our habits?

The reason we fail to accomplish it is that we are reluctant to accept change. There is a feeling of worry and uncertainty. We tend to focus on what-ifs.

Quite frequently, a lot of individuals spend their lives without embracing change, even if it leaves them unsatisfied and with some unmet aspirations.

But life is also about accepting change and taking on setbacks.

Organizational transformation is most successful when accompanied by good leadership. Leaders must plan for and adapt to change for the business and its people to prosper. I like change because it gives the chance to innovate, develop and fuel growth.

THE IMPORTANCE OF EMBRACING CHANGE

The primary concept of embracing change relates to establishing an attitude of accepting change as a good development and incorporating it into your life without fear. Change has three important advantages. It drives you to:LEARN NEW THINGS

MASTER NEW SKILLSBECOME WISER, FEARLESS AND ADAPTIVE.

Leaders understand these 4 principles of change to help organizations and their employees evolve and move to the next level of performance:

1. Change is Motivating:

We all heard the only certainty in life is death and taxes Q but you also need to add change. It's healthy and shows development is occurring. True leaders dont fear change; they embrace it with enthusiasm because they realize clever, motivated people grow in times of change .It also suggests that advancements are happening. A genuine leader is open to feedback from their team and appreciates ideas, no matter where they originated from. They are quick to praise and slow to chastise. Every new concept can render old ideas obsolete. The pain of the unknown is replaced by the exhilaration of discovery around the next bend.

2.Change is Exciting:

People spend an average of 40 hours a week at their employment. Some spend a lot more. The snooze button on the alarm clock is overused since it's quite simple for the daily routine to get tedious and monotonous .A good leader welcomes change to make work fresh and exciting for themselves and their team.

Think about your time at work. If it's not fun, do something about it now. Staff turnover is highly common in businesses where boredom flourishes. Keeping things new allows the firm to retain workers for longer periods of time.

3. Growth Only Happens when Things Change:
People and companies stagnate if they don't change. Personal and professional progress only occurs if changes are encouraged. Leaders grow better. Staff develop more abilities and become more confident. Followers are empowered to become leaders .Organizations gain from a financial and a personal point of view. Offices don't make a firm successful. Individuals are the engine for success and empowered people can practically achieve anything .

4. To Change is to Become Part of History:
Think back 5 or 50 years. Compare to today. There have been so many fantastic changes to the world we live in. These changes were created by individuals and groups of people who dared to take risks and question the status quo .The greatest approach to foresee the future is to

visualize it, then build it and invite others along for the trip. Space travel is now conceivable. Computers. Cellular phones. What was once solely in the imagination of a science fiction writer is now part of our everyday life. Scientific fiction meets science reality. It all starts with personal conviction and a single stride .

True leaders dont fear change. Nothing great is ever completed easily . But those who go on to accomplish tremendous heights would tell you that it was well worth the ride. Leaders accept change with open arms and are eager to venture into the void to explore what's out there a. Becoming a better leader is a tremendous incentive as we have seen thus often r.There is always a fine balance between status quo and change.
A great leader balances both and can make clear judgments when change is essential d. Once that is evident, it is necessary to respond fast and decisively. With the division of HP, this was quite clear. To drive the firm ahead, a big shift was necessary d. To make this successful, it

must be accompanied by a clear picture of what the change will accomplish ngLeaders have a crucial role when it comes to change. They must be prepared, exhibit personal dedication, and transmit a compelling vision.

Chapter 7

develop your workforce

Employee development is a process of strengthening workers' current competencies and abilities and establishing fresh ones to meet the organization's objectives.

Ways to grow your staff or employees

Start With Yourself:Before you can legitimately and successfully grow others, you need to develop yourself. Otherwise, you may come out as a hypocrite, rather than a true mentor. Shaping excellent conduct begins with role modeling, and understanding good self-development will also aid strengthen your talents in developing others.

Lay a Foundation of Trust and Mutual Respect:Employees need to realize that discussing their progress isn't simply a devious tactic to get them to acknowledge their faults. To motivate people to take ownership of the process, you have to start by developing trust.

Help them to know that you're involved in their achievement and on their side.

Turn Weekly Meetings Into Learning Opportunities:

Employee development isn't something that occurs solely in an annual review, nor something you can simply hand off to the HR department. All of your frequent contacts, from reviews, to project check-ins, to weekly meetings, are an opportunity to build your team. Consider methods to include a growth mentality in your regular meetings.

Ask Questions:Few individuals react well to merely being told what they need to accomplish. Instead of controlling the process, including your staff by asking smart questions. Coaching questions force workers to sort things out for themselves. Those inquiries may also be addressed after an assignment is finished as a means to reflect on lessons learned and reinforce the new knowledge or ability.

Learn How to Delegate:A lot of managers will spend time on a job that, although comfortable, they shouldn't be doing. Letting rid of the duties you love can help you grow your workers' talents and free up your time, so it's a win-win. But don't expect your reports to do things the same way you would do them. They may tumble at first and require further guidance, but that's how humans learn. They may ultimately accomplish the job better than you.

Give Stretch Tasks:Other than a job move, stretch assignments are hands down the finest method to learn and improve. As a manager, you're in a position to explore possibilities for your staff that is matched their development requirements and career objectives. Don't consider choosing the best competent individual for the task. Instead, consider finding the ideal developmental task for the individual.

Make Networking Introductions:Managers are frequently in the position to make introductions, open doors, and link workers to role models, subject-matter experts, and mentors. Expanding an employee's development network will reaffirm their ownership in the process and remind them that you're not the one that's ultimately accountable for their professional success. Besides, most likely someone helped open doors for you, so pay it forward whenever you can.

Feedback:We all have behavioral blind spots. A manager is frequently the individual who may delicately assist an employee realize a shortcoming that's standing in the way of their effectiveness or growth. Be prepared to provide comments not just during performance evaluations, but throughout the year.

Help Navigate Organizational Politics and Culture:Although "politics" is frequently considered a nasty term, it's the way things get done in companies. Your employees have to know this and learn to navigate the workplace culture. Job shadowing and role-playing are two methods to teach employees the ins and outs of being politically aware.

Spend Real Money:Lastly, wherever feasible, supplement your employee's growth objectives with training, conferences, coaches, and other real resources. An excellent training program, although not a replacement for what you can do as a manager, will boost your efforts and show your team members that you're involved in their advancement.

Benefits and relevance of employee development
A thoroughly thought-out personnel development plan is vital at numerous levels. And when successfully performed, it may yield various advantages to all parties involved, including workers, HR managers, and the larger business.
Some of these advantages include:
1. Performance Improvement

For organizations to stay competitive in their specialty, the organization must continue to exceed the competitors.
Employee development may help the business achieve – and even surpass – performance standards.

2. Better manage unforeseen circumstances
Today's corporate world is all about continual change. And that shift not only presents obstacles (for the workforce), but if managed appropriately, it also creates previously unanticipated possibilities. It is consequently crucial for the workforce to be able to manage ever-evolving circumstances promptly and efficiently.
Adaptable individuals are outstanding at inventing solutions when employees with less-developed talents would just accept the status quo.
One of the advantages of having a well-defined staff development program is that it helps prepare people to better manage the unexpected.

3. Learning culture within a business assists attract new workers and building loyalty

HR experts can relate to the fact that it's not simply enough to publicize job openings – it's equally crucial for potential workers to want to apply for those roles.

If the latter is lacking, organizations will not recruit the best and the brightest to help them stay competitive.

Helping develop employee talent, especially via strategies such as tailored development plans, produces a very desirable working environment.

According to the research such firms, that have a mature learning culture, are three times more likely to exploit that fact as a recruiting strategy. And developing a strong staff development program is the first step in that approach.

4. Save money by keeping personnel

Investing in in-house employee skills development programs is crucial to guarantee that the person can accomplish what they must do to "keep the ship afloat". However, staff development may also be a huge money-saver in the longer term.

It's crucial for organizations, at the top level, to engage and retrain personnel rather than always turning to the street to recruit.

5. Help grow potentially good employees into great leaders

If an organization wants to expand, survive and prosper in the long term, it has to generate a steady supply of would-be leaders.

6. Improve employee engagement and motivation with outstanding trainingHaving a staff that's completely dedicated and involved with the firm at every level is crucial for success. Driving employee engagement, so that they stay dedicated to the company's objective, is a consequence of numerous elements, such as a nice working environment, employee recognition and appreciation, regular communication, and effective training.

A well-defined employee engagement program may balance all the essential employee motivating variables, including training and skills development, to offer the advantages of a fully-motivated workforce throughout the firm.

7. This allows the organization freedom to develop, innovate and compete more fiercely within its specialty

To be a real market leader in one's area, organizations need to be agile, adaptable, and accommodating to the demands of their consumers and partners.

Having a well-balanced staff, that can innovate and compete for new business prospects, is one advantage that effective employee development programs give to firms.

Such programs not only strengthen current talents but may be utilized to provide longer-term competitiveness by teaching new skills that could be required in the future.

In summary, then, a well-trained, dynamic and highly motivated staff is vital to every firm. And the greatest approach to elevating personnel to such levels is to invest in their continual growth. Such personnel not only give financial advantages to the firm, in terms of profitability and performance gains but also assist with employee morale and retention.

Chapter 8

learn how to manage failure

We all have awful days and weeks when nothing seems to go right. We all have instances when we fail to attain something that we truly desired and find it hard to deal with.

However, some individuals appear considerably more able to pick themselves up and dust themselves off after these encounters than others.

One reason why some individuals find failure upsetting is because their identity is tied up with achieving.

In other words, when they fail, they regard themselves as a failure, rather than understanding that they have encountered a setback. As a leader try not to consider failure or success as personal: instead, it is something that you encounter. It does not alter the true 'you'.

As a workplace leader, you're counted on for more than merely driving initiatives and allocating responsibilities. Your workers count on you to establish a good, organized environment that encourages productivity and success.

Unfortunately, establishing a healthy workplace provides some of the largest, most complicated leadership problems you may encounter. If you're like most leaders today, you've experienced your fair share of problems and disappointments.

With so much uncertainty, change, and hostility in the job, the hardships you confront have probably never been higher. The idea is to learn from your mistakes and improve as a leader. If your leadership issues are affecting workplace morale, pulling down outcomes, or costing you workers, it's time to find out how to overcome the challenges you're encountering.

Here are 9 great tactics that are highly beneficial in overcoming setbacks and setbacks on the way to success.

1. Take Responsibility for your failures.

No one likes to fail yet expecting that you will never fail is absurd. Taking responsibility for your role in a failure is a chance to learn and do better or differently next time.

2. Take time to analyze a setback.

After facing a setback, know that you will need some time to comprehend what just occurred to you. There is no defined length of time to recover from a failure so don't feel you have to hurry the process.

3. Give yourself a break and vary things up.

Obsessing about your setback is simply going to keep you stranded. Try to do something pleasant, walk outside, take a vacation from social media and simply give your mind a rest. It's hard to recover if you continue to keep focused on your setback.

4. Reflect with trustworthy colleagues and mentors.

When you've encountered a failure, ask a trustworthy coworker or mentor for their honest input. Good mentors will offer you genuine comments, let you vent, and provide the support and encouragement to help you take great strides ahead.

5. Create contingency plans.

When making future choices, consider the probable difficulties that may come and prepare for them. Being proactive and having a contingency plan at the ready for when difficulties emerge can benefit you enormously.

6. Determine what's in your control.

Think about what you have within your control. If you failed due to a lack of information or abilities, take a course or do some more reading to learn extra skills to position yourself for success in the future.

7. Try New methods.

Be adaptable and open-minded to testing new ways. Some leaders become rigid and excessively cautious following a setback. Taking chances is crucial for leaders who want to achieve. Don't cocoon yourself or be frightened of making choices, you will make more correct ones than bad ones.

8. Be determined and positive.

Be careful to retain a positive mindset no matter how hard this may be. This is particularly vital if you are a leader. If your firm stops and your workers are scared about losing their jobs, they will turn to you for leadership and assurance that things will get better.

9. Reframe and Reflect to keep on track.

I've mentored countless company executives who retain notes and look back on them periodically as a method of keeping themselves on track so as not to make the same errors moving ahead.

While setbacks and barriers may derail us, they also provide chances to look at a situation from a different viewpoint. Failures force us to learn and acquire confidence in our talents and judgment. Many professional and personal breakthroughs have been accomplished after a failure has happened. Persevering through setbacks can assist you – and your business – to continue to develop and flourish.

Printed in Great Britain
by Amazon

16058372R00047